W9-AOA-092

MIDLOTHIAN
PUBLIC LIBRARY

GET IN THE GAME

Snap books

A GIRL'S GUIDE TO

★ SOFTBALL ★

by Janelle Valido Woodyard

Consultant:
Suzy Brazney
Head Softball Coach, Golden West College
Huntington Beach, California

CAPSTONE PRESS
a capstone imprint

Snap Books are published by Capstone Press,
1710 Roe Crest Drive, North Mankato, Minnesota 56003
www.capstonepub.com

Books published by Capstone Press are manufactured with paper
containing at least 10 percent post-consumer waste.

Library of Congress Cataloging-in-Publication Data
Woodyard, Janelle Valido.
 A girl's guide to softball / by Janelle Valido Woodyard.
   p. cm. — (Snap books. Get in the game.)
Includes bibliographical references and index.
Summary: "Quizzes, rules, and tips and tricks on how to play softball"—Provided by publisher.
ISBN 978-1-4296-7672-4 (library binding)
1. Softball for women—Juvenile literature. I. Title.
GV881.3.W66 2012
796.357'8082—dc23   2011036702

Editor: Mari Bolte
Designer: Bobbie Nuytten
Media Researcher: Eric Gohl
Production Specialist: Laura Manthe

Photo Credits: Capstone Studio/Karon Dubke, 5, 13, 17, 19, 22 (bottom), 23, 25, 27, 29; Fotolia/Actionpics, 12;
Getty Images/John Giustina, cover (bottom right); iStockphoto/AVAVA, 20; Newscom/Icon SMI/J.P. Wilson, 26,
Icon SMI/William Purnell, 10, ZUMA Press, 9; Shutterstock/Alex Staroseltsev, cover (top left), back cover, 2,
4–5 (top), 24–25 (top), Jean Schweitzer, 22 (top), kanate, 8, Levente Gyori, 24, Lori Carpenter, 21, saiko3p, 16
(bottom), Sportlibrary, 6, Steve Cukrov, 7, Wendy Nero, 11, 15, Yuri Samsonov, 16 (top)

Design Elements
Shutterstock/Sergey Kandakov (stars); Solid (cheering crowd)

Printed in the United States of America in North Mankato, Minnesota.
102011   006405CGS12

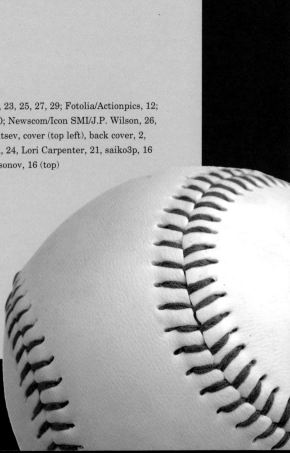

TABLE OF CONTENTS

CHAPTER 1 ★

Take the Quiz!

Do you love to chase down fly balls? Can you slap the ball through the infield or hit the ball out of the park? Can you run the bases like your feet are on fire? Or maybe you'd rather cheer for your favorite team from the stands. You're not alone! Girls around the world get together to throw, hit, slide, run, and catch. Take a crack at this quiz to figure out your softball know-how.

1. The difference between fastpitch and slowpitch softball is:

a) the pitching distance is different

b) the pitching technique is different

c) there are a different number of players on the field

d) all of the above

2. You're pitching your first fastpitch game. How far do you have to throw the ball?

a) 43 feet (13 meters)

b) 50 feet (15.2 m)

c) 35 feet (10.7 m)

d) 40 feet (12.2 m)

3. You're running the bases and are almost to second. The second base player is getting ready to catch the ball. It's going to be close! You should:

a) tackle the girl playing second

b) touch second base and keep going to third

c) slide to reach the base faster

d) turn around and run back to first

4. You're on third base and are ready to run to home. Your teammate hits a fly ball. The third base coach reminds you to tag up. What does she mean?

a) You should let yourself get tagged.

b) You should not leave the base until the fly ball is caught.

c) You should not leave the base until the ball is thrown.

d) Give your teammates a high-five if you score a run.

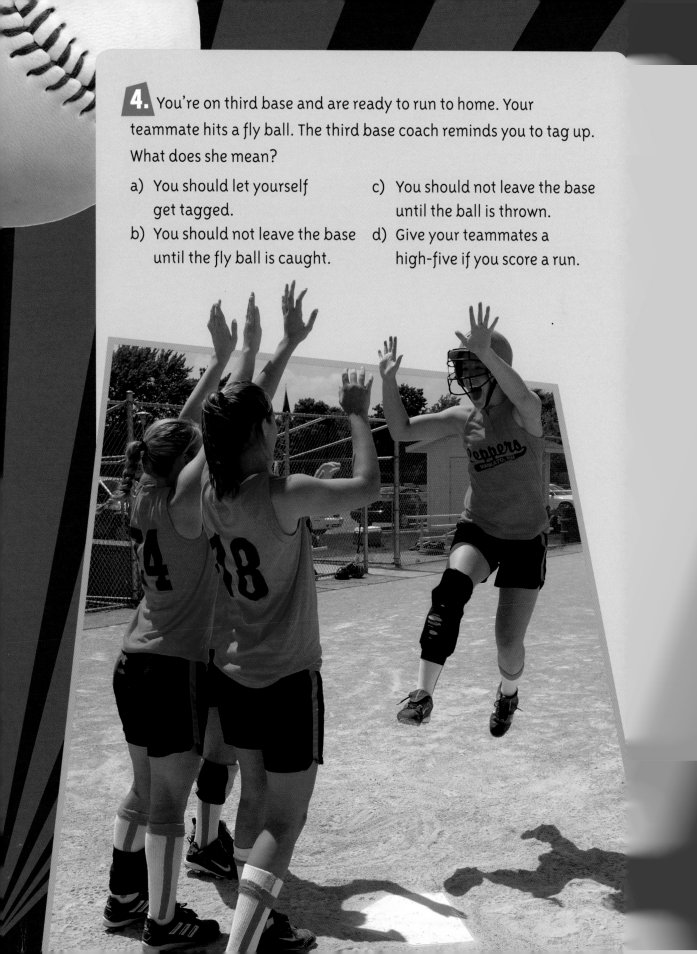

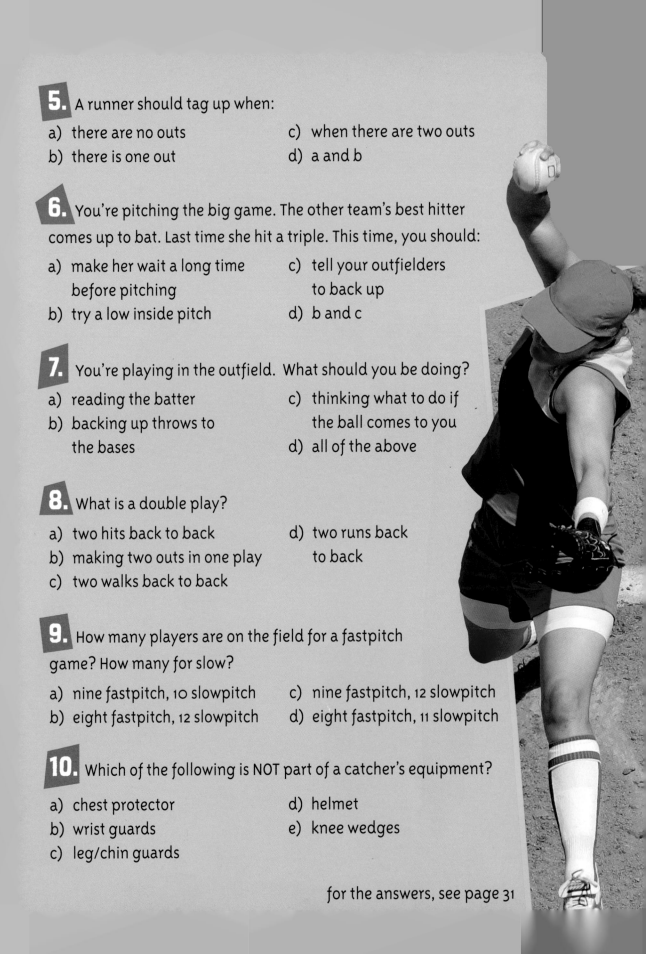

5. A runner should tag up when:

a) there are no outs

b) there is one out

c) when there are two outs

d) a and b

6. You're pitching the big game. The other team's best hitter comes up to bat. Last time she hit a triple. This time, you should:

a) make her wait a long time before pitching

b) try a low inside pitch

c) tell your outfielders to back up

d) b and c

7. You're playing in the outfield. What should you be doing?

a) reading the batter

b) backing up throws to the bases

c) thinking what to do if the ball comes to you

d) all of the above

8. What is a double play?

a) two hits back to back

b) making two outs in one play

c) two walks back to back

d) two runs back to back

9. How many players are on the field for a fastpitch game? How many for slow?

a) nine fastpitch, 10 slowpitch

b) eight fastpitch, 12 slowpitch

c) nine fastpitch, 12 slowpitch

d) eight fastpitch, 11 slowpitch

10. Which of the following is NOT part of a catcher's equipment?

a) chest protector

b) wrist guards

c) leg/chin guards

d) helmet

e) knee wedges

for the answers, see page 31

CHAPTER 2

Know the Rules

Before you join a team, you need to decide what kind of game you want to play. Would you pick fastpitch or slowpitch? Fastpitch requires nine players, including a powerful pitcher. During a fastpitch game, the pitcher tries to strike out the other team's batters. Balls whiz over home plate at speeds greater than 50 miles (80 kilometers) per hour. Slowpitch balls cross the plate at slower speeds and are thrown in an arc. As you might guess, it's easier to hit a slowpitch ball! But that doesn't mean it's easier to score runs. Slowpitch teams have 10 players on the field. That's one more person in the outfield just waiting to get you out.

No matter which type of softball you play, the basic game is the same. The home team jogs onto the field to play defense. The visiting team gathers by its dugout and gets ready to bat. The two teams switch places after three outs. Once each team has had a chance to bat, the inning is over. The team with the most runs after seven innings wins.

The team taking the field is divided into infielders and outfielders. They do whatever it takes to get three outs and keep the other team from scoring runs.

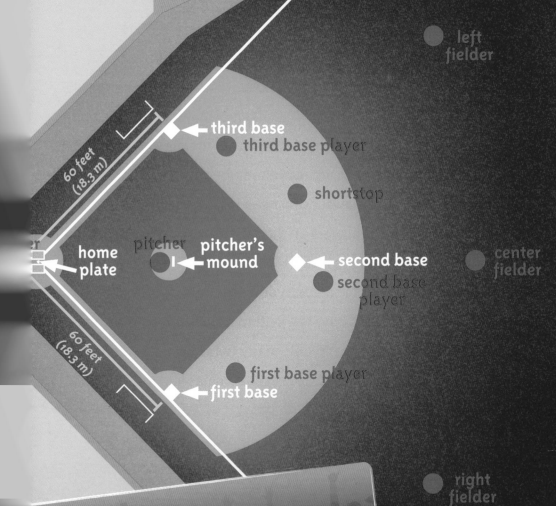

Fastpitch pitchers stand 43 feet (13 meters) from home plate. Slowpitch pitchers are 50 feet (15.2 m) away.

foul line

left fielder

60 feet (18.3 m)

third base

third base player

shortstop

pitcher

home plate

pitcher's mound

second base

second base player

center fielder

60 feet (18.3 m)

first base player

first base

right fielder

Tip: Are you left-handed? Try playing first base. You might find it more comfortable to field the ball from first base than other positions.

THE INFIELDERS: Do you like being in the middle of the action? Then head to the infield! If you're playing first base, you've got to be great at catching the ball. You'll need to stretch if you're going to tag the other team's base runner out.

Second base players need to be fast on their feet. The ball could come flying by on either the left or the right. A skilled player can move from side to side with ease.

If you're the shortstop, you've got to be ready for anything. Can you stop a fast-moving grounder? Can you get under pop flies? Can you lend support to your teammates at second base and third base? Then shortstop is the position for you!

To play third base, you need to have quick reactions to catch hard hits, low grounders, and line drives. You also need a strong arm to throw the ball across the infield to first base.

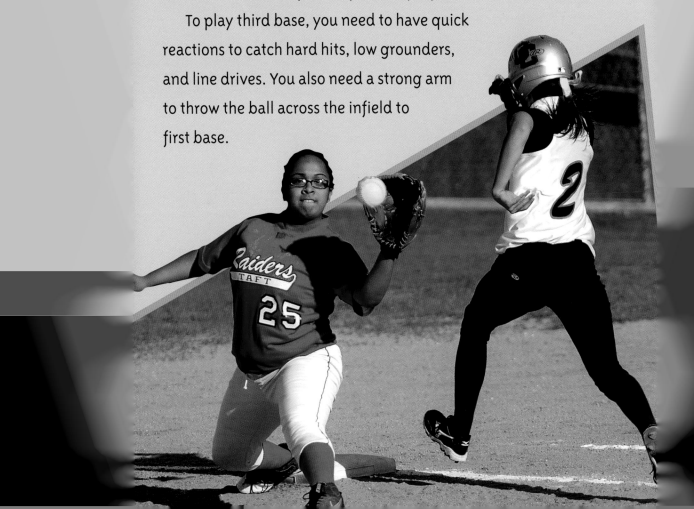

THE OUTFIELDERS: If you have a strong arm and can throw the ball quickly and accurately, you belong in the outfield! The outfielders are positioned in the grass behind the infield. Choose from left field, center field, and right field.

Outfielders are constantly moving. The ball could end up bouncing lazily down a baseline or soaring out of the park. They also support the infielders. Generally, the left fielder backs up third base. The center fielder backs up second base. She also helps out the shortstop. And the right fielder helps out at first base.

THE PITCHER: Pitching is both a physical and mental position. A good pitcher needs to watch the base runners and know the number of outs. She also has to choose the pitches that will strike out the other team's batters. And she needs to be able to play the game from beginning to end. A good pitcher can't sweat mistakes made in the first inning. There are six more innings to go!

All softball pitchers throw underhand, but the pitching speed varies. Fastpitch pitchers play to strike out the other team's batters. They can control where the ball crosses the plate. And their pitches are fast! The pitcher's throwing arm rotates in a full 365-degree circle around her shoulder for maximum speed. The pros can throw pitches around 65 miles (105 km) per hour.

In slowpitch, the ball is thrown in a more gentle arc. The arc needs to be between 6 and 12 feet (1.8 and 3.7 m) high. Strikeouts in slowpitch are rare.

THE CATCHER: Teamwork between the pitcher and catcher is important. The catcher suggests pitches to the pitcher. And she watches the rest of the field. Got a runner trying to steal second base? A fast throw from the catcher to the shortstop and that runner is out!

A great catcher needs physical, mental, and leadership skills. She needs to be able to throw long distances with accuracy. She needs to know the rules of the game and call plays. And she needs to be able to communicate with the umpire, if necessary.

The catcher wears a helmet and face mask, a chest protector, and shin guards. She also wears knee wedges. These are cushions that protect the catcher's knees. Since the catcher spends most of the game crouching, the wedges also help reduce knee stress.

The first rule of softball is to keep your eye on the ball. Whether the pitcher throws a drop ball, rise ball, or curveball, you need to be prepared. Keep the bat loose and your body balanced. Decide which stance you'll use. A closed stance places the batter's front foot closer to home plate. In an open stance, the batter's rear foot is closer. A square stance means both feet are the same distance from the plate. Choosing the stance that works best for you will ensure maximum hitting power. And when you hit the ball, run for first!

Once you're on base, be a smart base runner. Keep an eye on both the pitcher and the catcher. Listen to your base coaches, but don't be afraid to think for yourself. Watch where your teammates hit the ball, and make the right choices.

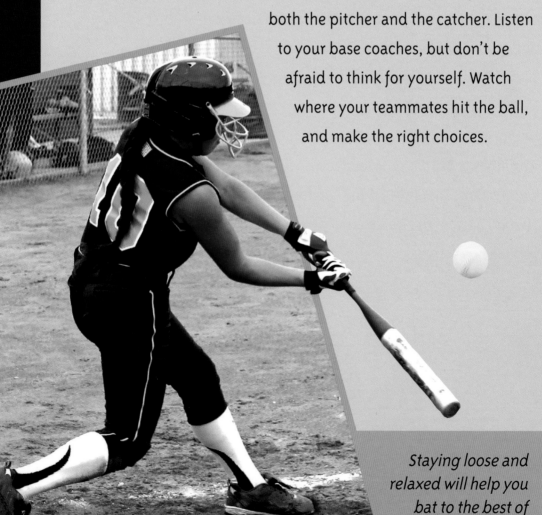

Staying loose and relaxed will help you bat to the best of your ability.

Here are a few tips on when to run and when to stay put:

- If the batter hits a ground ball, run for it!

- If the batter hits a pop fly, watch to see if it's caught. If the ball hits the ground, run for the next base. Be ready to slide if the play is going to be close.

- If the batter hits a pop fly and it is caught, you'll have to make a quick decision. You can stay on your base or tag up after the catch and advance to the next base. Prepare to slide!

The Bent-Leg Slide

You're running toward the next base. The infielder is ready to catch the ball and tag you out. You'd better slide! About 15 feet (4.6 meters) before reaching the base, stretch one leg straight out. Bend the other leg at the knee.

Tuck your bent leg behind your straight leg in the shape of a 4. As your feet begin sliding toward the base, lean back. You should lay flat and low to the ground. This posture makes it hard for the other player to tag you. If you're lucky, you'll beat the ball.

CHAPTER 3 ★

Playing Your Best

Playing softball works both your upper and lower body. Every throw, catch, and swing builds muscle in your upper body. Those movements increase your body's **flexibility** and strength.

Softball girls are constantly running, bending, sprinting, and shuffling. All that movement is great for the lower body. Exercise causes your blood to flow faster. The increased blood flow strengthens your muscles and bones. It also keeps your body healthy.

Think of the times you're running on and off the field. All that running gets your heart racing. Playing softball is a good way to strengthen your heart and lungs. Increased **stamina** will improve your game and benefit both you and your team.

A fit body means nothing if you can't make the parts work together. Softball players need great hand-eye **coordination**. It takes special skills to catch a line drive, drill the ball through the infield, and hit a home run. The brain, hands, and eyes all work together to get the job done.

FLEXIBILITY: the ability to bend or move easily

STAMINA: the energy and strength to keep doing something for a long time

COORDINATION: the ability to control body movements

The faster you can run, the greater chance you'll have of beating the ball!

A healthy body performs best, so take care of yourself. Get plenty of sleep and eat right. A balanced diet will help fuel your body both on and off the field. **Carbohydrates**, **protein**, and potassium give your body energy. The **calories** in carbohydrates fuel the body. Foods, such as whole grain bread, pasta, and cereal, are full of good carbohydrates.

Protein is especially important for any athlete. The **nutrients** you get from protein strengthen and repair your body's muscles. Lean meats, eggs, and fish are great protein choices.

Potassium sends oxygen to your brain, which keeps you alert. It also helps your body avoid muscle cramps. Leafy vegetables, oranges, bananas, and sunflower seeds are good sources of potassium.

CARBOHYDRATE: a substance that gives you energy

PROTEIN: a substance found in foods such as meat, cheese, eggs, and fish

CALORIE: a measurement of the amount of energy that food gives you

NUTRIENT: a substance needed by a living thing to stay healthy

Make sure you're drinking enough water to prevent **dehydration**. Drink plenty of water before, during, and after the game. Your muscles tire when your body runs out of water. So drink early and often.

Sports drinks are OK but can be full of sugar and empty calories. Water is all-natural and has no calories or fat. If you take care of your body, your body will take care of you.

DEHYDRATION: a life-threatening medical condition caused by a lack of water

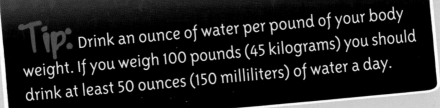

Tip: Drink an ounce of water per pound of your body weight. If you weigh 100 pounds (45 kilograms) you should drink at least 50 ounces (150 milliliters) of water a day.

BALLPARK CRUNCH

Are you looking for a snack that scores with your teammates? Try this tasty little treat. It's great on and off the field and will help get your energy levels back to where they belong.

INGREDIENTS

8 cups (1,920 milliliters) air-popped popcorn, from about ⅓ cup (80 mL) kernels
¼ cup (60 mL) almonds
3 cups (720 mL) mini marshmallows

2 tablespoons (15 mL) butter
¼ cup (60 mL) peanut butter
food coloring
edible glitter (optional)

SUPPLIES

large mixing bowl
microwave-safe bowl
spoon

pot holders
cooking spray

Step 1: Measure and pour popcorn and almonds into the large bowl. Toss lightly to mix.

Step 2: Measure and pour marshmallows, butter, and peanut butter into microwave-safe bowl.

Step 3: Microwave marshmallow mixture for 30 seconds. Stir. Repeat until marshmallow mixture is completely melted. Use pot holders to remove bowl from microwave.

Step 4: Add food coloring to marshmallow mixture until it's your desired color.

Step 5: Pour marshmallow mixture over the popcorn. Stir until popcorn is evenly coated.

Step 6: Spray your hands with cooking spray. Shape popcorn into balls.

Step 7: Sprinkle popcorn balls with edible glitter for some sparkle 'n shine.

Tip: Don't have an air popper? Use a 5-ounce (142-gram) bag of lightly salted microwave popcorn instead.

Tip: The food coloring will cause the marshmallow mixture to firm up. Don't worry, it's supposed to do that!

CHAPTER 4 ★

Improve Your Game

No matter how good you are, there's always room for improvement. Could your hand-eye coordination use some work? What about your batting? Maybe you could be more physically fit. Play catch with a friend to improve your reaction time and glove handling. To up your batting game, try hitting balls of different sizes and weights. Go for a swim, take a run, or learn some new dance moves to improve your fitness.

Softball is a game of speed and strength. Hitting, running bases, and moving in to catch the ball all require quick, explosive power. These skills require **core strength**. A strong core will allow a player to run, jump, and bat all day. Pull-ups, crunches, and push-ups are great exercises to build core strength. Try working out with an exercise ball for an added core boost.

Running bases is hard on the knees. Sprinting and sliding place strain on the body's **ligaments**. Throwing and catching are hard on the wrist and shoulder. Hips and elbows are also common areas for injury. Having a strong body will help minimize strain on your joints.

CORE STENGTH: development of the abdominal and back muscles

LIGAMENT: a band of tissue that connects or supports bones and joints

Even when softball isn't in season, it's essential to keep your body active. Walking, running, and biking are excellent and easy ways to get off the couch. But there are other, more creative, ways to stay in shape. Canoeing, kayaking, or rowing will work your upper body. Horseback riding, skateboarding, or skiing will work your legs and core. Or cross-train by trying karate, yoga, or pilates.

To sharpen your skills, be on the lookout for softball camps or workshops in your area. Having someone new see your softball skills is a great way to take your abilities to the next level. They won't know your abilities so they will be able to see your strengths and weaknesses. And getting tips from a pro can never hurt!

Staying Loose

Staying strong is important to playing well. But softball players spend most of the game standing or sitting. Not moving can cause muscles to cool down and react slower. This can be a problem when the ball comes your way and you need to move quickly! And pulled muscles aren't the only thing players need to worry about.

One way to avoid stressing your body is to stay warmed up. Even if you stretch properly before the game, standing in the outfield can cool down your muscles. Cool muscles are much more prone to injury. So be sure to move around and stretch when you can.

CHAPTER 5 ★

Working Together

There's more to softball than a strong arm or a great swing. Softball is a team sport. Without a team, you'd have no game! Teammates who know one another have an easier time playing together. They know one another's strengths and weaknesses. And they trust one another to make the right plays.

There are a lot of different ways to get to know your teammates. Get together before the game to get energized. Make decorations for your clothes, bedrooms, or lockers that show off your team spirit. Wear team gear off the field to let people know you're a team. During the game, cheer each other on. Create a secret handshake or a team cheer to use on the field. Whether you win or lose, your team will stick together.

Tip: Participating in sports has been proven to lead to success later in life. On average, athletic kids have better attendance records, higher grades, and lower drop-out rates. They are also more active overall.

Even after the softball season is over, there are many ways to get together as a team. Sign up for a summer team to keep your skills sharp. Volunteer to help coach a Little League team. Visit the batting cages or just go out and play catch. Or lace up your tennis shoes and hit the trail. Run relays or just jog as a group.

If you need a break from playing the game, why not watch? Go see the pros play in a stadium. Or invite everyone over to watch the big game on TV. Singing "Take Me Out to the Ballgame" has never been so fun!

You can stay fit with your friends without picking up a bat too. Join a gym and work out together. Sign up for yoga or pilates and go as a group. Grab your suits to go for a swim. Work on your teamwork while playing a different sport. Try basketball, hockey, or soccer. Cross-training will keep your body moving and your friendships fresh.

If you're switching activities, why not try something completely different? Attend a cooking class together or try out for a community play. Learn to knit or start on a team scrapbook. Then bring your signature recipe, song, or hand-knitted hats to your next game!

Anything you can do as a team is a step toward creating a strong, healthy, happy bond. Not only will you have lots of fun, you also make lasting friendships with other softball lovers!

TEAM SEAMS

Make an accessory that will show off your softball spirit. Personalize it with buttons, puffy paint, or cords in your team colors. Get the girls together so everyone can make one!

WHAT YOU'LL NEED:

pencil
1.75 inch-wide (4.4 centimeter-wide) strip of white vinyl fabric (or craft leather) long enough to circle your wrist
ruler
1.75 inch-wide (4.4 cm-wide) strip of felt the same length as the vinyl strip

craft knife
⅛-inch (.3 cm) hole punch
two 30-inch (76-cm) pieces red waxed cotton cord
button with a shank
fabric glue

Step 1: Use a pencil to lightly mark two centered dots at each end of the vinyl. The dots should be about ¼-inch (.6 cm) from the edge of the fabric.

Step 2: Using the ruler as a guide, draw a straight line down the center of the vinyl. The line should end ¼-inch (.6 cm) before the dots.

Step 3: Use the craft knife to carefully cut through the straight line.

Step 4: Lightly mark 15 evenly-spaced dots along each side of the center cut.

Step 5: Punch out the 30 dots and the dots at the ends of the bracelet.

Step 6: Line the cords up end to end. Thread the cords through the button's shank. Center the button on the cords.

Step 7: Thread the cords through the bracelet's end holes. Pull so the button is tight against the bracelet.

Step 8: Lace the cords by pulling one end through a hole and under the bracelet's center line. Continue until bracelet is fully laced. Trim and knot the ends of the cords. Leave the ends long enough to tie around the button.

Step 9: To hide the knots, glue the felt to the back of the vinyl. Let dry before wearing.

GLOSSARY

calorie (KA-luh-ree)—a measurement of the amount of energy that food gives you

carbohydrate (kar-boh-HYE-drate)—a substance found in foods such as bread, rice, cereal, and potatoes that gives you energy

coordination (koh-OR-duh-nay-shun)—the ability to control body movements

core strength (KOR STRENGKTH)—development of the abdominal and back muscles that surround the core area of the body

dehyration (dee-hy-DRAY-shuhn)—a life-threatening medical condition caused by a lack of water

flexibility (FLEK-suh-bil-uh-tee)—the ability to bend or move easily

ligament (LIG-uh-muhnt)—a band of tissue that connects or supports bones and joints

nutrient (NOO-tree-uhnt)—a substance needed by a living thing to stay healthy

protein (PROH-teen)—a substance found in foods such as meat, cheese, eggs, and fish

stamina (STAM-uh-nuh)—the energy and strength to keep doing something for a long time

READ MORE

Lockman, Darcy. *Softball For Fun!* Sports For Fun. Minneapolis: Compass Point Books, 2006.

Schwartz, Heather E. *Girls' Softball: Winning on the Diamond.* Girls Got Game. Mankato, Minn.: Capstone Press, 2007.

Wesley, Ann. *Competitive Fastpitch Softball For Girls.* Sports Girl. New York: Rosen Central, 2001.

INTERNET SITES

FactHound offers a safe, fun way to find Internet sites related to this book. All of the sites on FactHound have been researched by our staff.

Here's all you do:

Visit *www.facthound.com*

Type in this code: 9781429676724

  Check out projects, games and lots more at
www.capstonekids.com

QUIZ ANSWERS: 1. d 2. a 3. c 4. b 5. d 6. d 7. d 8. b 9. a 10. b

INDEX